D1318765

The
Sleepy Time
Treasury

The Sleepy Time Treasury

compiled by Dale Payson ★ Karen Maxwell Wyant
pictures by Dale Payson

Prentice-Hall ★ *Englewood Cliffs* ★ *N.J.*

Printed in the United States of America • J

Prentice-Hall International, Inc., London
Prentice-Hall of Australia, Pty. Ltd., North Sydney
Prentice-Hall of Canada, Ltd., Toronto
Prentice-Hall of India Private Ltd., New Delhi
Prentice-Hall of Japan, Inc., Tokyo

Library of Congress Cataloging in Publication Data
Main entry under title:
The sleepy time treasury.
  SUMMARY: A collection of traditional and contemporary poems for bed and naptime.
  1. Sleep—Juvenile poetry. [1. Sleep—Poetry]
I. Payson, Dale. II. Wyant, Karen.
PZ8.3.S6324   821'.008'0355   75–11624
ISBN 0–13–812891–X

Acknowledgments

"Grown-Up" by Dorothy Aldis: Reprinted by permission of G. P. Putnam's Sons from FAVORITE POEMS OF DOROTHY ALDIS by Dorothy Aldis. Copyright © 1970 by Roy E. Porter.

"Shop of Dreams" by Mary Jane Carr: Copyright © 1941 by Mary Jane Carr; from the book, TOP OF THE MORNING, published by Thomas Y. Crowell. Reprinted by permission of the author and McIntosh and Otis, Inc.

"Far Away" by Elizabeth Coatsworth: Reprinted from THE SPARROW BUSH by Elizabeth Coatsworth. Copyright © 1966 by Grosset & Dunlap, Inc.

"The Mouse" by Elizabeth Coatsworth: Reprinted by permission of Coward McCann & Geoghegan, Inc. from COMPASS ROSE by Elizabeth Coatsworth. Copyright 1929 by Coward-McCann, Inc., renewed 1957 by Elizabeth Coatsworth.

"Where" by Walter de la Mare: Reprinted by permission of The Literary Trustees of Walter de la Mare, and The Society of Authors as their representative.

"Bedtime" by Eleanor Farjeon: Copyright 1933, © renewed 1961 by Eleanor Farjeon. From POEMS FOR CHILDREN by Eleanor Farjeon. Copyright 1951 by Eleanor Farjeon. Reprinted by permission of J. B. Lippincott Company.

Table of Contents

The Man in the Moon   9
  Anonymous
This Is My Rock   10
  David McCord
Slumber Song   12
  Louis V. Ledoux
The Snail   14
  James Reeves
The Sugar-Plum Tree   17
  Eugene Fields
Nighttime   20
  Nina Payne

Come, Let's to Bed   22
  Anonymous
Falling Star   25
  Sara Teasdale
Bedtime   26
  Aileen Fisher
Grown-up   29
  Dorothy Aldis
Bedtime   30
  Eleanor Farjeon
The Night   33
  Myra Cohn Livingston
My Stay-Awake Schemes   34
  Barbara Joy Albanese
Finis   36
  Sir Henry Newbolt

The Little Girl Lost   39
   Barbara Taylor Bradford
Crescent Moon   40
   Elizabeth Madox Roberts
Bed in Summer   43
   Robert Louis Stevenson
The Night Watchmen   44
   Wymond Garthwaite
Where   47
   Walter de la Mare
The Mouse   48
   Elizabeth Coatsworth
Willie Winkie   51
   Anonymous
Far Away   52
   Elizabeth Coatsworth

The Sandman   55
   Barbara Taylor Bradford
The Lullaby Lady   56
   Loryn Parker
Shop of Dreams   58
   Mary Jane Carr
Last Song   60
   James Guthrie

The Man in the Moon

The Man in the Moon looked out of the moon,
Looked out of the moon and said,
" 'Tis time for all children on the earth
To think about getting to bed!"

9

This Is My Rock

This is my rock,
And here I run
To steal the secret of the sun;

This is my rock,
And here come I
Before the night has swept the sky;

This is my rock,
This is the place
I meet the evening face to face.

DAVID MC CORD

Slumber Song

Drowsily come the sheep
From the place where the pastures be,
  By a dusty lane
  To the fold again,
First one, and then two, and three:
  First one, then two, by the paths of sleep
  Drowsily come the sheep.

Drowsily come the sheep,
And the shepherd is singing low:
  After eight comes nine
  In the endless line,
They come, and then in they go.
  First eight, then nine, by the paths of sleep
  Drowsily come the sheep.

Drowsily come the sheep
And they pass through the sheepfold door;
   After one comes two,
   After one comes two,
Comes two and then three and four.
   First one, then two, by the paths of sleep,
   Drowsily come the sheep.

               LOUIS V. LEDOUX

13

The Snail

At sunset, when the night-dews fall,
Out of the ivy on the wall
With horns outstretched and pointed tail
Comes the grey and noiseless snail.
On ivy stems she clambers down,
Carrying her house of brown.
Safe in the dark, no greedy eye
Can her tender body spy,
While she herself, a hungry thief,
Searches out the freshest leaf.
She travels on as best she can
Like a toppling caravan.

JAMES REEVES

14

The Sugar-Plum Tree

Have you ever heard of the Sugar-Plum Tree?
   'Tis a marvel of great renown!
It blooms on the shore of the Lollipop sea
   In the garden of Shut-Eye Town;
The fruit that it bears is so wondrously sweet
   (As those who have tasted it say)
That good little children have only to eat
   Of that fruit to be happy next day.

When you've got to the tree, you would have a hard time
   To capture the fruit which I sing;
The tree is so tall that no person could climb
   To the boughs where the sugar-plums swing!
But up in that tree sits a chocolate cat,
   And a gingerbread dog prowls below—
And this is the way you contrive to get at
   Those sugar-plums tempting you so:

You say but the word to that gingerbread dog
   And he barks with such terrible zest
That the chocolate cat is at once all agog,
   As her swelling proportions attest.
And the chocolate cat goes cavorting around
   From this leafy limb unto that,
And the sugar-plums tumble, of course, to the ground—
   Hurrah for that chocolate cat!

There are marshmallows, gumdrops, and peppermint canes,
   With stripings of scarlet or gold,
And you carry away of the treasure that rains
   As much as your apron can hold!
So come, little child, cuddle closer to me
   In your dainty white nightcap and gown,
And I'll rock you away to that Sugar-Plum Tree
   In the Garden of Shut-Eye Town.

EUGENE FIELDS

18

Nighttime

Wrapped up by the night
It's cold
Where there are no lights on
I know everyone in sight
I'm warm
I've got my flipflops on

My Poppa's going to read a book
To me
It's one I know by heart
I do not need to look
To see
He's coming to the scary part

20

And when I go to bed
I'll dream
But I don't know which kind
Just somewhere in my head
I'll hear
The stories that are on my mind.

NINA PAYNE

21

Come, Let's to Bed

"Come, let's to bed,"
  says Sleepy-head;
"Tarry a while," says Slow.
"Put on the pan,"
  says Greedy Nan,
"Let's sup before we go."

The Falling Star

I saw a star slide down the sky,
Blinding the north as it went by,
Too burning and too quick to hold,
Too lovely to be bought or sold,
Good only to make wishes on
And then forever to be gone.

SARA TEASDALE

25

Bedtime

Ladybugs haven't a house to sweep
or a bed to make or a yard to keep,
so at night
they stay where they are to sleep,
on a twig or leaf or stem.

Butterflies, folding their wings up tight,
sleep in the grass when day turns night,
down where it's dark
and out of sight,
down near the meadow's hem.

Bumblebees hurry when day is through
to crawl in a blossom pink or blue
or yellow or white,
and fragrant too . . .
I'd rather sleep like them.

AILEEN FISHER

Grown-Up

I'm growing up, my mother says—
Today she said I'd grown;
The reason why is this: Now I
Can do things all alone.

And though I'm glad that I don't need
Someone to brush my hair
Or wash my hands and face and button
Buttons everywhere.

Although I'm very glad indeed
To help myself instead,
I hope that I won't have to try
TO TUCK MYSELF IN BED!
                    DOROTHY ALDIS

Bedtime

Five minutes, five minutes more, please!
  Let me stay five minutes more!
Can't I just finish the castle
  I'm building here on the floor?
Can't I just finish the story
  I'm reading here in my book?
Can't I just finish this bead-chain—
  It *almost* is finished, look!
Can't I just finish this game, please?
  When a game's once begun
It's a pity never to find out
  Whether you've lost or won.
Can't I just stay five minutes?
  Well, can't I stay just four?
Three minutes, then? two minutes?
  Can't I stay *one* minute more?

ELEANOR FARJEON

The Night

The night
  creeps in
  around my head
  and snuggles down
  upon the bed,
  and makes lace pictures
  on the wall
  but doesn't say a word at all.

MYRA COHN LIVINGSTON

33

My Stay-Awake Schemes

Riding a horse on a dusty trail,
   Guiding a boat with a great big sail;
Rolling down a hill of green,
   Splashing through a sparkling stream;
A shaggy dog with a cold wet nose,
   A fire that warms the fingers and toes;
A twinkling star, shining bright,
   To wish upon in the dark, dark night;
Something to nibble before going to bed,
   Like jelly or jam or honey on bread;
These are some of the plans I make
   When thinking of reasons for staying awake.

Morning comes; I open my eyes,
  And I find out to my surprise
That what I thought were stay-awake schemes
  Were really part of my sleepy-time dreams.

BARBARA JOY ALBANESE

Finis

Night is come,
   Owls are out;
Beetles hum
   Round about.

Children snore
   Safe in bed;
Nothing more
   Need be said.
         SIR HENRY NEWBOLT

The Little Girl Lost

They found her sleeping in the snow
A lost little girl they did not know.
"She must be cold," cried the tiny gnomes
And so they built her a house of cones.
The deer came by with a piece of fur
Which made a warm coverlet for her.
They sewed the bag of winds up tight
And asked the moon to shine very bright.
All the night they watched her one by one
Until the morning brought out the sun.
Of course they had gone when she awoke
Those gentle, friendly forest folk.

BARBARA TAYLOR BRADFORD

39

Crescent Moon

And Dick said, "Look what I have found!"
And when we saw we danced around,
And made our feet just tip the ground.

We skipped our toes and sang, "Oh-lo.
Oh-who, oh-who, oh what do you know!
Oh-who, oh-hi, oh-loo, kee-lo!"

We clapped our hands and sang, "Oh-ee!"
It made us jump and laugh to see
The little new moon above the tree.

ELIZABETH MADOX ROBERTS

Bed in Summer

In winter I get up at night
And dress by yellow candle-light.
In summer, quite the other way,
I have to go to bed by day.

I have to go to bed and see
The birds still hopping on the tree,
Or hear the grown-up people's feet
Still going past me in the street.

And does it not seem hard to you,
When all the sky is clear and blue,
And I should like so much to play,
To have to go to bed by day?

ROBERT LOUIS STEVENSON

Night Watchmen

When I'm in bed at night,
  Outside my door
And just in sight
At the head of the stairs
Sit two little bears.

They sit very still,
  As still as can be.
They're sitting on guard,
  Just watching, you see.

Their ears are wide open,
  And so are their eyes,
They'll catch anyone
  If anyone tries
To come up the stairs.
But nobody dares
Because of the bears!

WYMOND GARTHWAITE

Where

Monkeys in a forest,
Beggarmen in rags,
Marrow in a knucklebone,
Gold in leather bags;

Dumplings in the oven,
Fishes in a pool,
Flowers in the parlour,
Dunces in a school;

Feathers in a pillow,
Cattle in a shed,
Honey in a beehive,
   And me in bed.

WALTER DE LA MARE

The Mouse

I heard a mouse
Bitterly complaining
In a crack of moonlight
Aslant on the floor—

"Little I ask,
And that little is not granted;
There are few crumbs
In this world any more.

"The bread box is tin
And I cannot get in.

"The jam's in a jar
My teeth cannot mar.

"The cheese sits by itself
On the ice-box shelf.

"All night I run
Searching and seeking;
All night I run
About on the floor.

"Moonlight is there
And a bare place for dancing,
But no little feast
Is spread any more."

ELIZABETH COATSWORTH

48

Willie Winkie

Wee Willie Winkie runs through the town,
Upstairs and downstairs in his night-gown,
Rapping at the window, crying through the lock,
Are the children all in bed, for now it's eight o'clock?

Far Away

Once a little boy
  Lived with a bear,
Went to sleep
  Against deep, brown hair,
Warm and safe
  In a hidden lair,

Gathered berries
  Where wild fruits grow,
Drank from cold streams
  Born of the snow,
Stared down at valleys
  Far below.

Though he at last
  Returned to men,
And never walked
  With the bears again,
All his life long
  He dreamed of the den.

ELIZABETH COATSWORTH

The Sandman

The Sandman has the swiftest wings
And shoes that are made of gold,
He calls on you as the first star sings
When the night is not very old.

He carries a tiny silver spoon
And a bucket made of night,
He fills your eyes with bits of moon
And stardust that's shiny and bright.

He takes you on a ship that sails
Through the land of dreams and joys,
And tells you many wondrous tales
Of dragons and magical toys.

So come now and rest your sleepy head
And close your eyes very tight,
For should you stay awake instead
The Sandman won't pass by tonight.

BARBARA TAYLOR BRADFORD

The Lullaby Lady

Have you heard of the Lullaby Lady,
Who lives on a cloud, snowy white;
Where she sits making songs for the children,
By the rays of the moon, all the night?

Now, of course, she could never send Tommy
A song that was meant for a Joan,
So you see she must be really careful
To play each a song of his own.

And after the lullaby's finished,
A nightingale takes it away,
And whispers it softly and sweetly
To Mummy, while you are at play.

Then when you are tucked up so snugly,
Your Mummy will hum out aloud
The song that the Lullaby Lady
Made up for you on the white cloud.

LORYN PARKER

56

Shop of Dreams

Shop of dreams is up on a hill,
   Close to the morning star;
An odd little shop, in a meadow of sleep,
   Where all kinds of novelties are.

Just follow the road to Slumberland,
   That leads over hill and dale,
And right at the end you will see a sign:
   "Very Fine Dreams For Sale."

The keeper of dreams is an old, old man,
  With a twinkle in his eye—
He's been showing his wares
    since the world was new,
  To people who come to buy;

Tucked under the eaves, small drowsy birds
  Sing slumber songs, over and over,
While wooly white sheep jump over the fence
  To nibble the moonbeam clover.

MARY JANE CARR

59

Last Song

To the Sun
Who has shone
  All day,
To the Moon
Who has gone
  Away,
To the milk-white
Silk-white,
Lily-white Star
A fond goodnight
Wherever you are.
       JAMES GUTHRIE

Index

Bed in Summer   43
   Robert Louis Stevenson

Bedtime   30
   Eleanor Farjeon

Bedtime   26
   Aileen Fisher

Come Let's to Bed   22
   Anonymous

Crescent Moon   40
   Elizabeth Madox Roberts

Falling Star   25
   Sara Teasdale

Far Away   52
   Elizabeth Coatsworth

Finis   36
   Sir Henry Newbolt

Grown-up   29·
   Dorothy Aldis

Last Song   60
   James Guthrie

Little Girl Lost, The   39
   Barbara Taylor Bradford

Lullaby Lady, The   56
   Loryn Parker

Man in the Moon, The   9
   Anonymous

Mouse, The   48
   Elizabeth Coatsworth

My Stay-Awake Schemes   34
  Barbara Joy Albanese

Night, The   33
  Myra Cohn Livingston

Nighttime   20
  Nina Payne

Night Watchmen, The   44
  Wymond Garthwaite

Sandman, The   55
  Barbara Taylor Bradford

Shop of Dreams   58
  Mary Jane Carr

Slumber Song   12
  Louis V. Ledoux

Snail, The   14
  James Reeves

Sugar-Plum Tree   17
  Eugene Fields

This Is My Rock   10
  David McCord

Where   47
  Walter de la Mare

Willie Winkie   51
  Anonymous

INDEX OF FIRST LINES

And Dick said, "Look what I have found!"   40

At sunset, when the night-dews fall,   14

"Come, let's to bed,"   22

Drowsily come the sheep   12

Five minutes, five minutes more, please!   30

Have you ever heard of the Sugar-Plum Tree?   17

Have you heard of the Lullaby Lady,   56

I heard a mouse   48

I saw a star slide down the sky,   25

I'm growing up, my mother says—   29

In winter I get up at night   43

Ladybugs haven't a house to sweep   26

Monkeys in a forest,   47

Night is come,   36

Once a little boy   52

Riding a horse on a dusty trail,   34

Shop of dreams is up on a hill,   58

The Man in the Moon looked out of the moon,   9

The night   33

The Sandman has the swiftest wings   55

They found her sleeping in the snow   39

This is my rock,   10

To the Sun   60

Wee Willie Winkie runs through the town,   5

When I'm in bed at night,   44

Wrapped up by the night   20